FOR ORGANS, PIANOS & ELECTRONIC KEYBOARDS

E-Z PLAY TODAY

279

ALAN JACKSON

PRECIOUS MEMORIES

 T0069339

ISBN-13: 978-1-4234-2780-3

 HAL•LEONARD®
CORPORATION

7777 W. BLUEMOUND RD. P.O. BOX 13819 Milwaukee, WI 53213

E-Z Play® Today Music Notation © 1975 by HAL LEONARD CORPORATION

E-Z PLAY and EASY ELECTRONIC KEYBOARD MUSIC are registered trademarks of HAL LEONARD CORPORATION.

Visit Hal Leonard Online at
www.halleonard.com

Blessed Assurance

Registration 6
Rhythm: Waltz

Lyrics by Fanny J. Crosby
Music by Phoebe Palmer Knapp

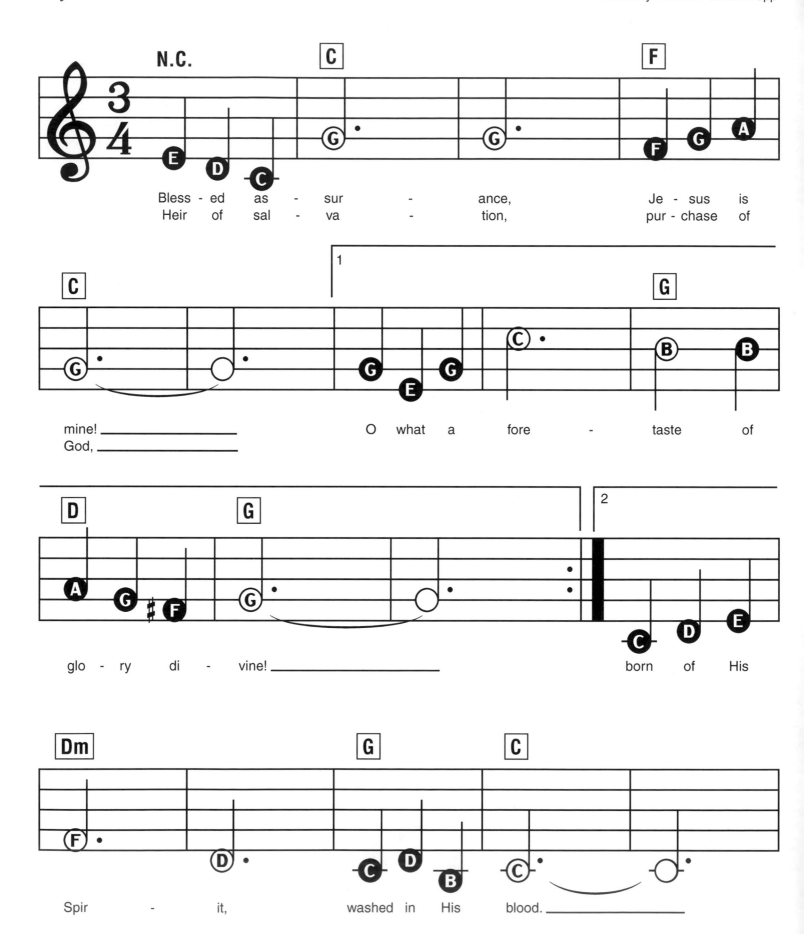

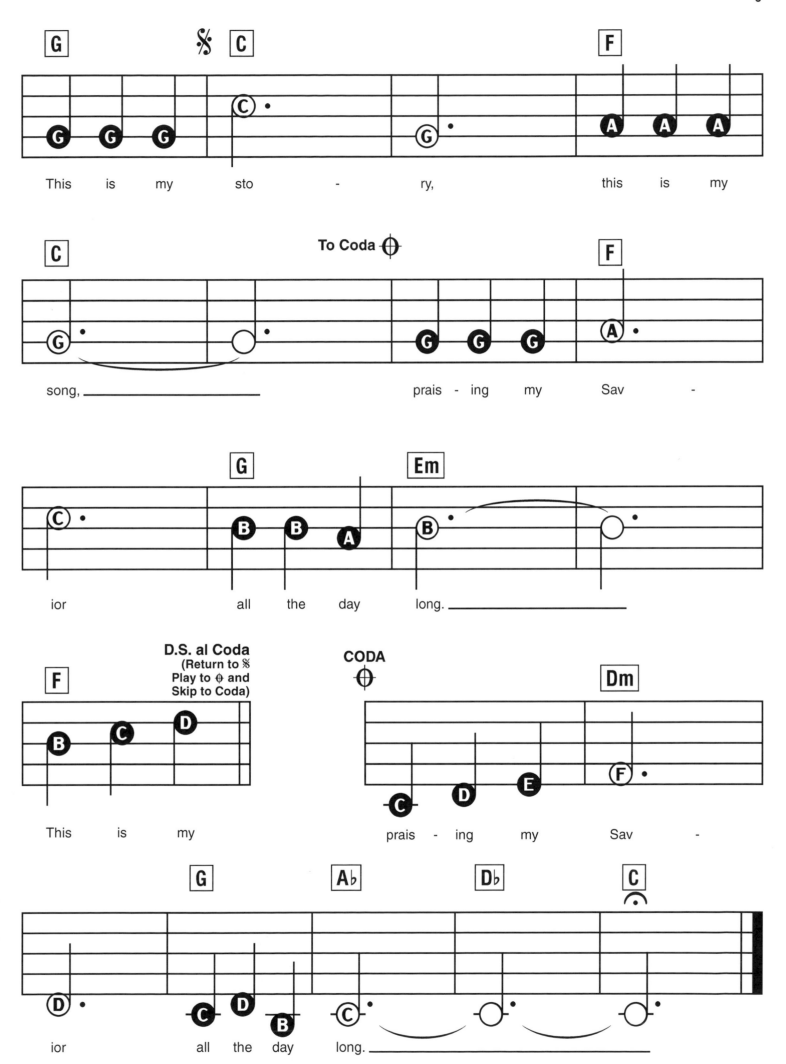

Softly and Tenderly

Registration 1
Rhythm: Waltz

Words and Music by
Will L. Thompson

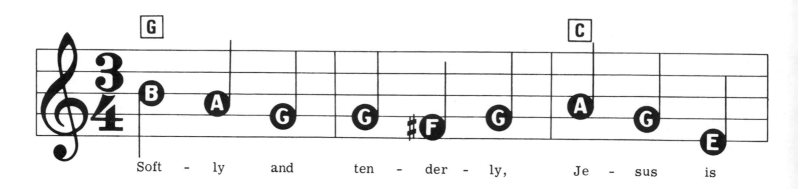

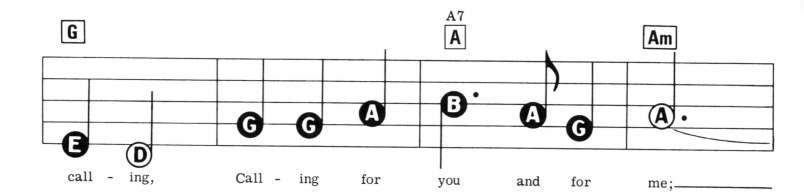

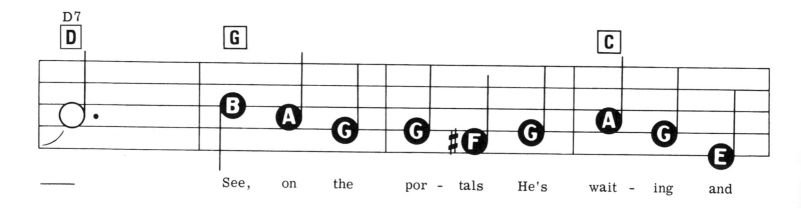

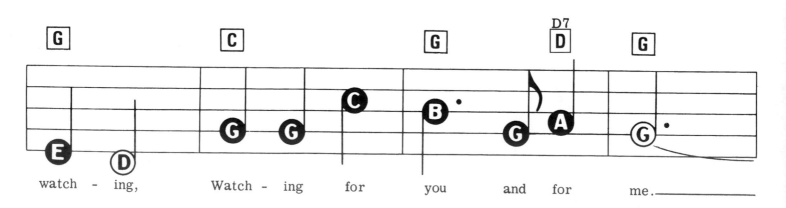

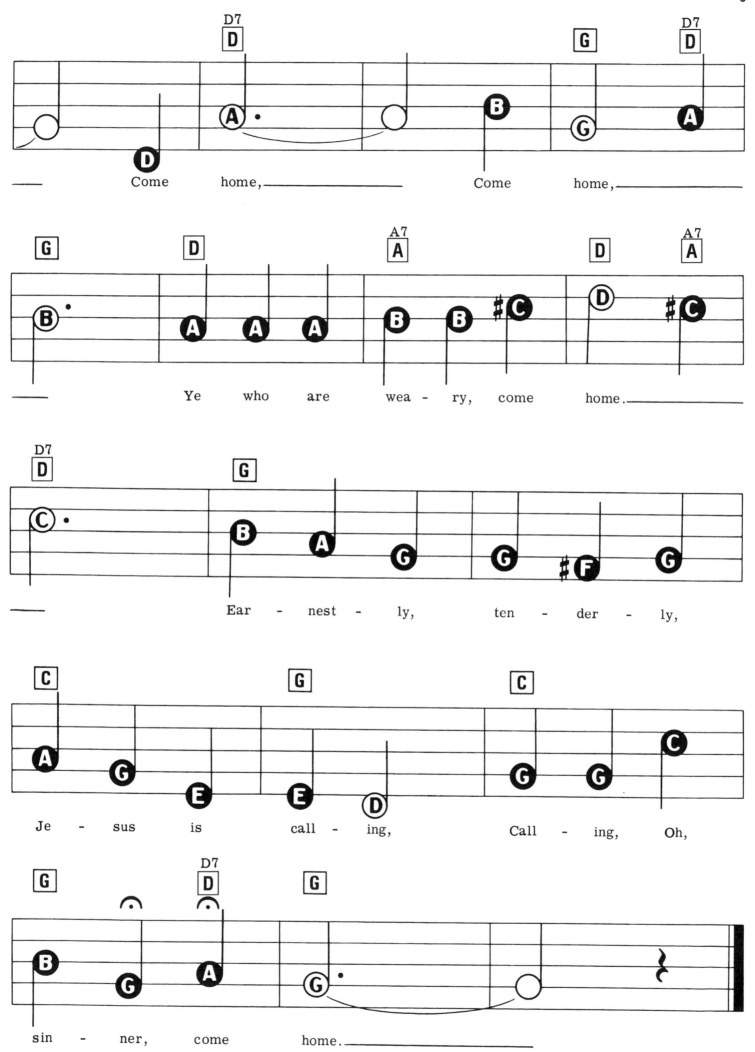

I Love to Tell the Story

Registration 4
Rhythm: March

Words by A. Catherine Hankey
Music by William G. Fischer

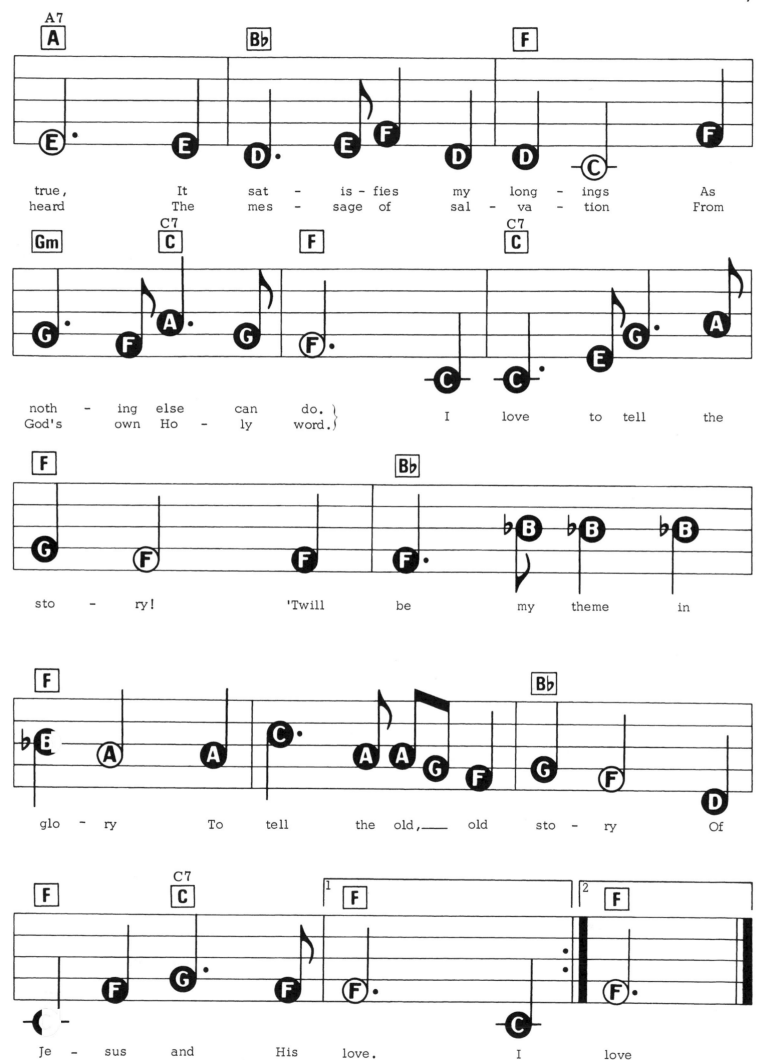

When We All Get To Heaven

Registration 4
Rhythm: Ballad or Fox Trot

Words by Eliza E. Hewitt
Music by Emily D. Wilson

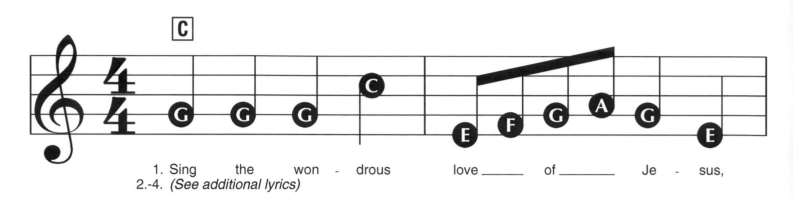

1. Sing the won - drous love _____ of _____ Je - sus,
2.-4. *(See additional lyrics)*

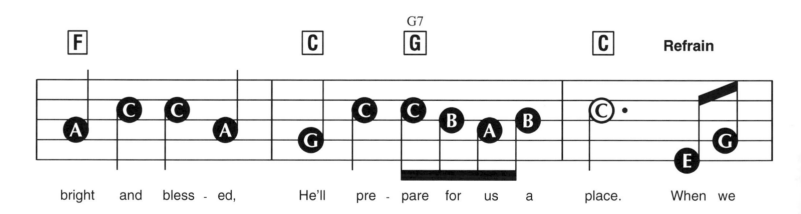

sing His mer - cy _____ and His grace. In the man - sions,

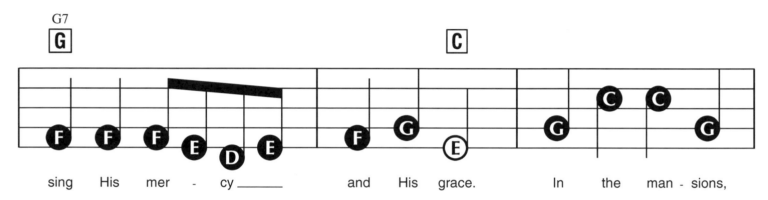

bright and bless - ed, He'll pre - pare for us a place. When we

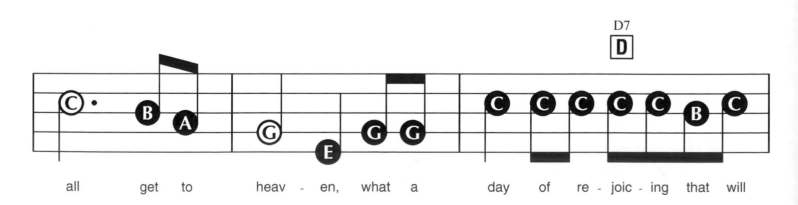

all get to heav - en, what a day of re - joic - ing that will

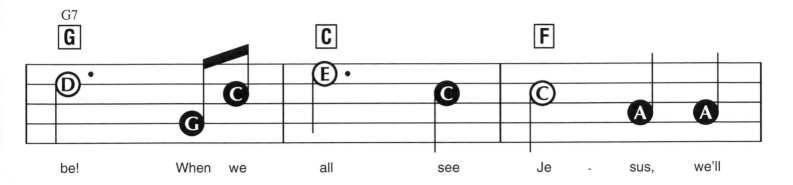

be! When we all see Je - sus, we'll

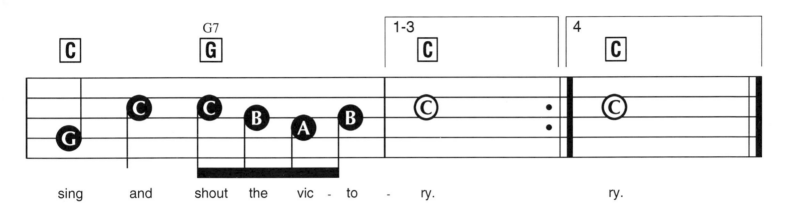

sing and shout the vic - to - ry. ry.

Additional Lyrics

2. While we walk the pilgrim pathway
   Clouds will overspread the sky;
   But when trav'ling days are over,
   Not a shadow, not a sigh!
   Refrain

3. Let us then be true and faithful,
   Trusting, serving ev'ryday;
   Just one glimpse of Him in glory
   Will the toils of life repay.
   Refrain

4. Onward to the prize before us,
   Soon His beauty we'll behold!
   Soon the pearly gates will open,
   We shall tread the streets of gold.
   Refrain

'Tis So Sweet to Trust in Jesus

Registration 1
Rhythm: Fox Trot

Words by Louisa M.R. Stead
Music by William J. Kirkpatrick

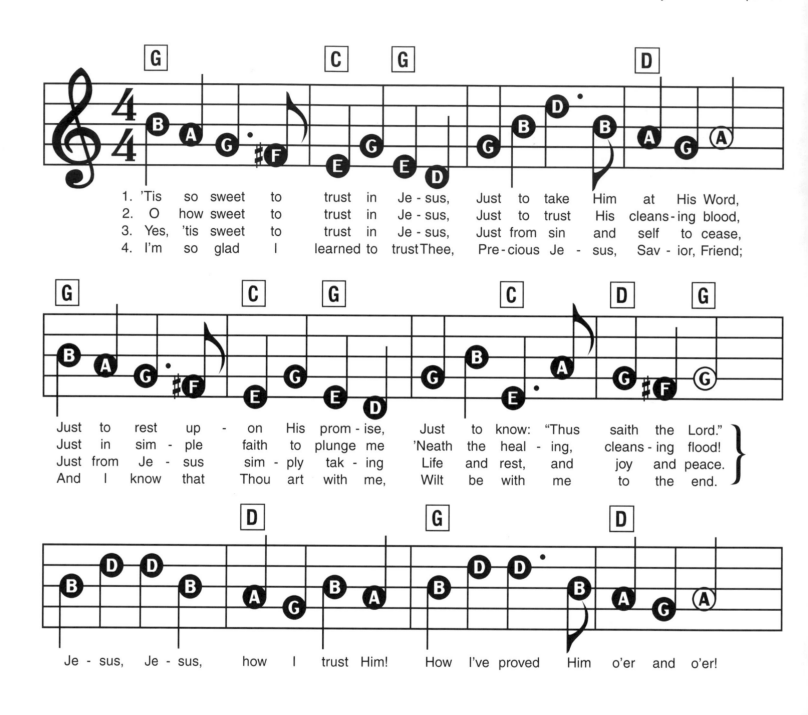

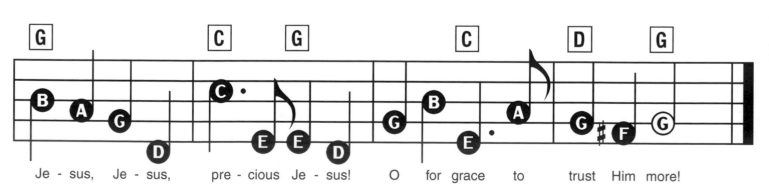

I'll Fly Away

Registration 4
Rhythm: Country or Fox Trot

Words and Music by
Albert E. Brumley

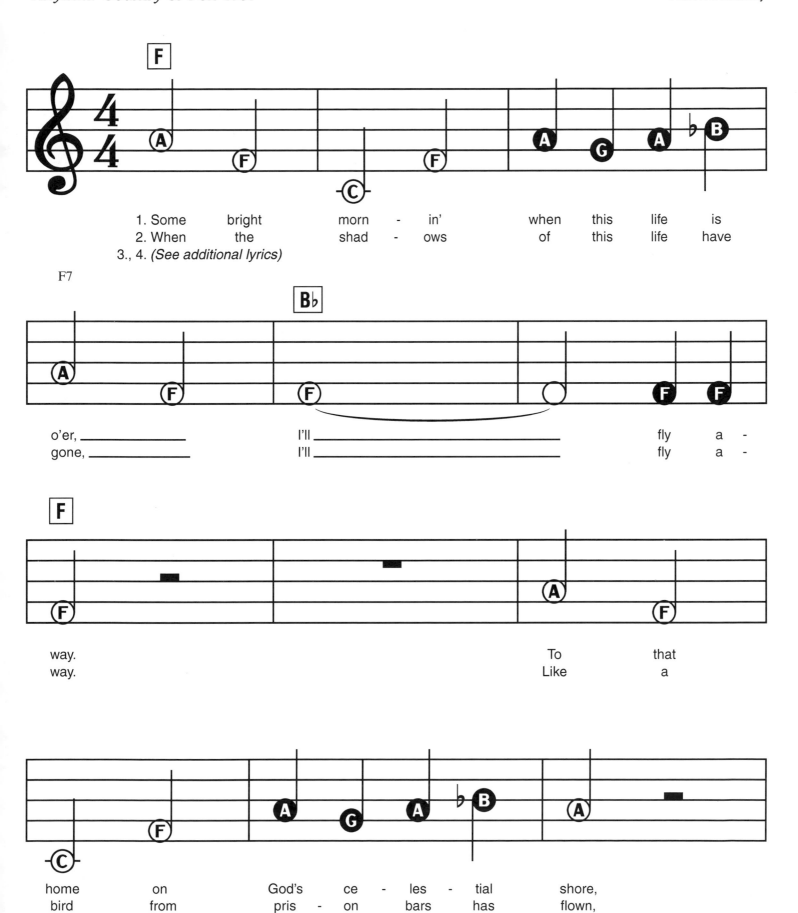

1. Some bright morn - in' when this life is
2. When the shad - ows of this life have
3., 4. *(See additional lyrics)*

o'er, _____ I'll _____ fly a -
gone, _____ I'll _____ fly a -

way.   To that
way.   Like a

home on God's ce - les - tial shore,
bird from pris - on bars has flown,

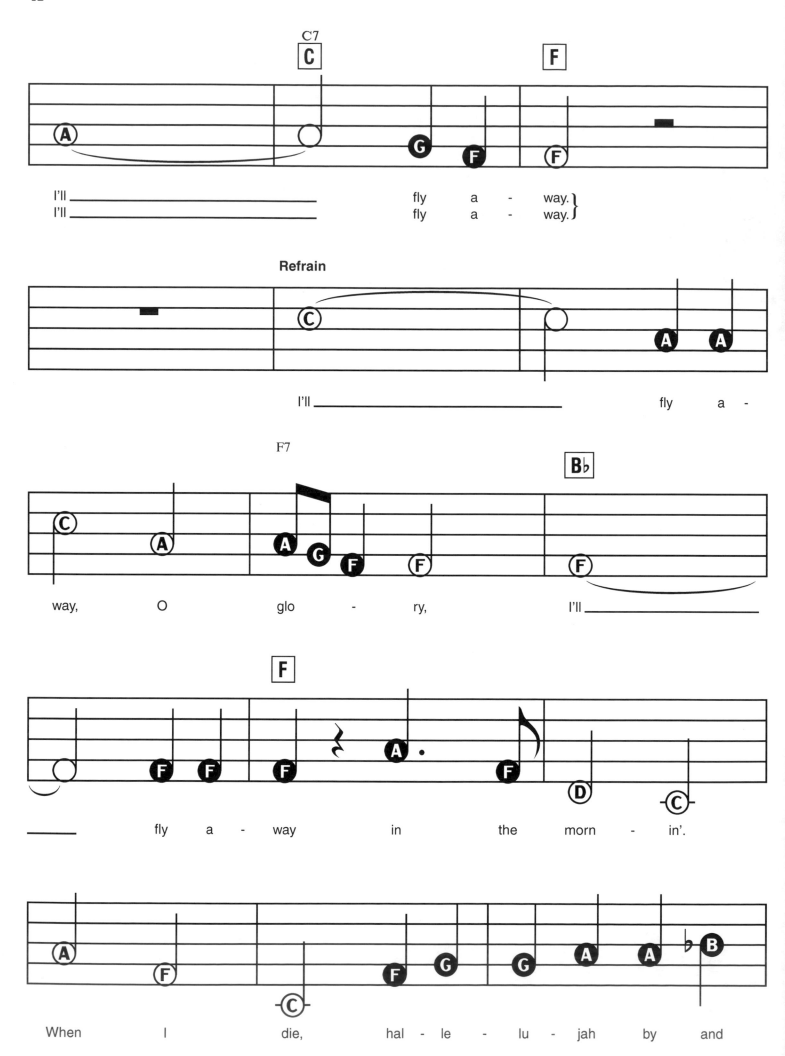

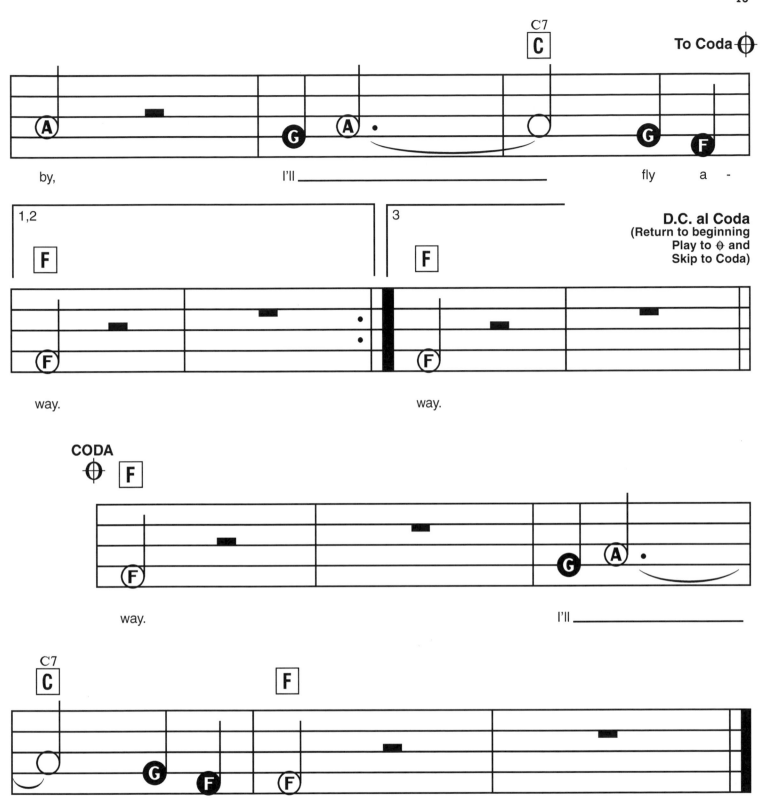

Additional Lyrics

3. Oh, how glad and happy when we meet,
   I'll fly away.
   No more cold iron shackles on my feet,
   I'll fly away.
   Refrain

4. Just a few more weary days and then
   I'll fly away
   To a land where joys will never end,
   I'll fly away.
   Refrain

In the Garden

Registration 2
Rhythm: Waltz

Words and Music by
C. Austin Miles

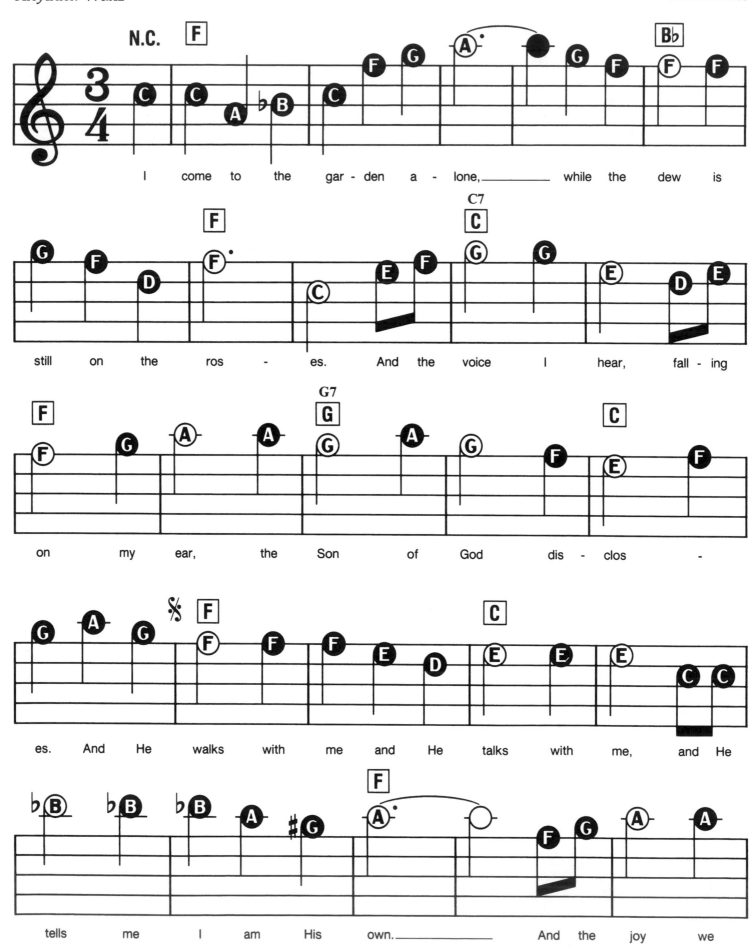

15

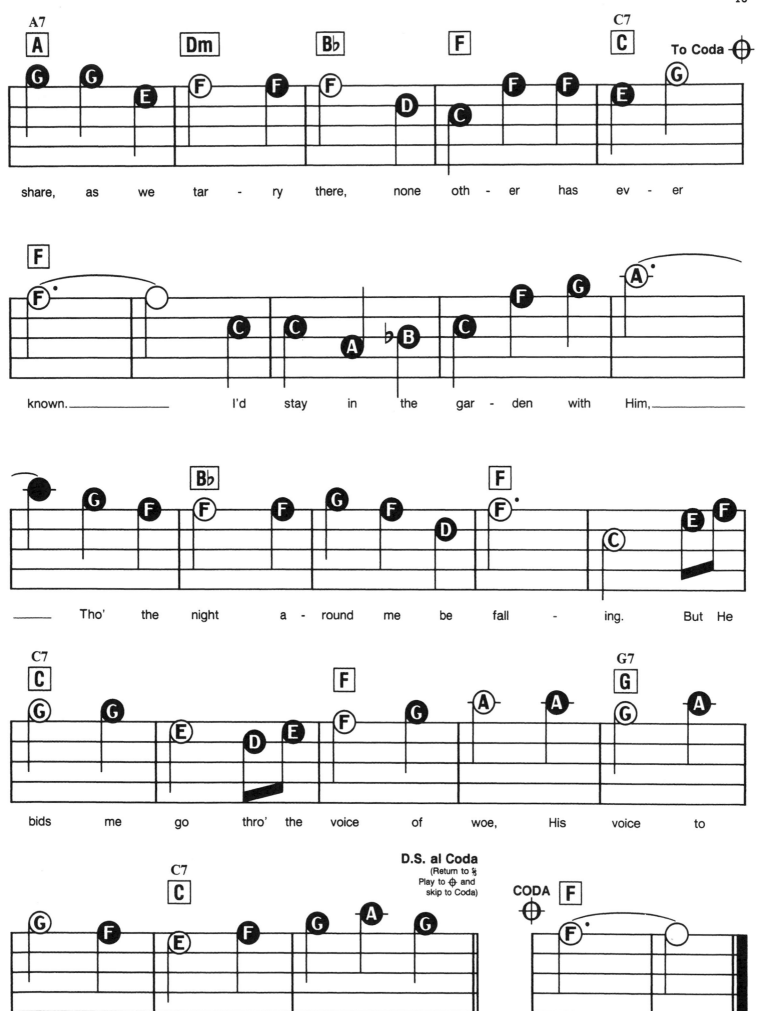

Are You Washed in the Blood?

Registration 2
Rhythm: Ballad or Fox Trot

Words and Music by
Elisha A. Hoffman

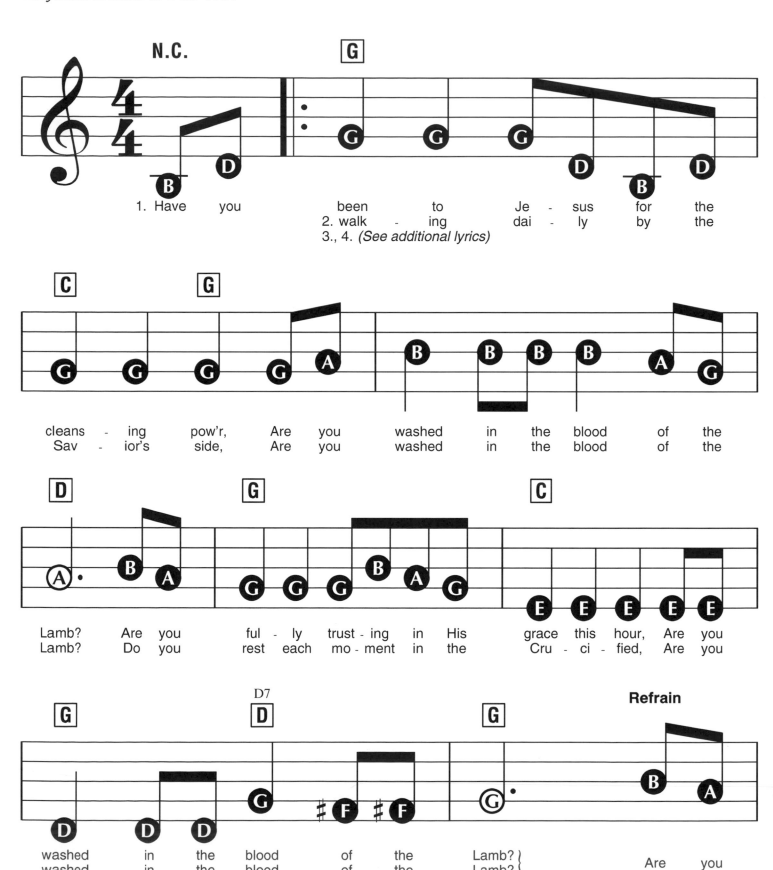

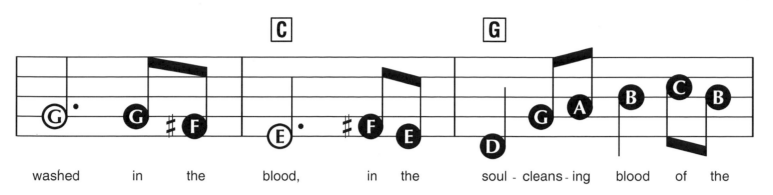

washed in the blood, in the soul - cleans - ing blood of the

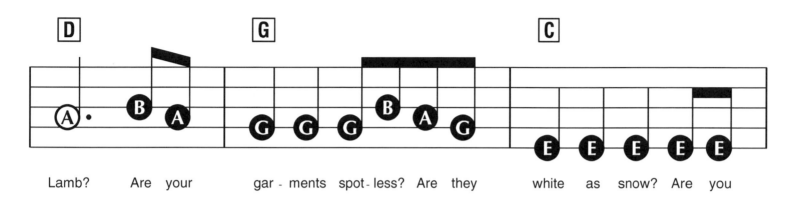

Lamb? Are your gar - ments spot - less? Are they white as snow? Are you

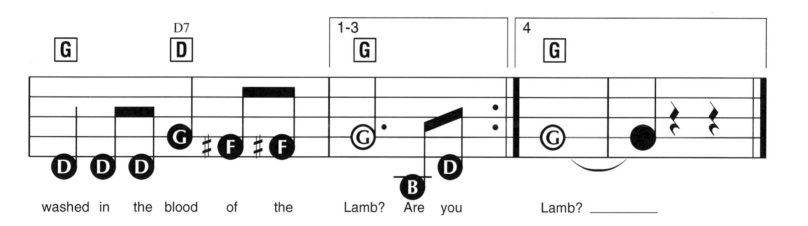

washed in the blood of the Lamb? Are you Lamb? _____

Additional Lyrics

3. When the Bridegroom cometh will your robes be white,
   Are you washed in the blood of the Lamb?
   Will your soul be ready for the mansions bright
   And be washed in the blood of the Lamb?
   Refrain

4. Lay aside the garments that are stained with sin,
   And be washed in the blood of the Lamb,
   There's a fountain flowing for the soul unclean,
   O be washed in the blood of the Lamb!
   Refrain

What a Friend We Have in Jesus

Registration 8
Rhythm: Fox Trot

Words by Joseph M. Scriven
Music by Charles C. Converse

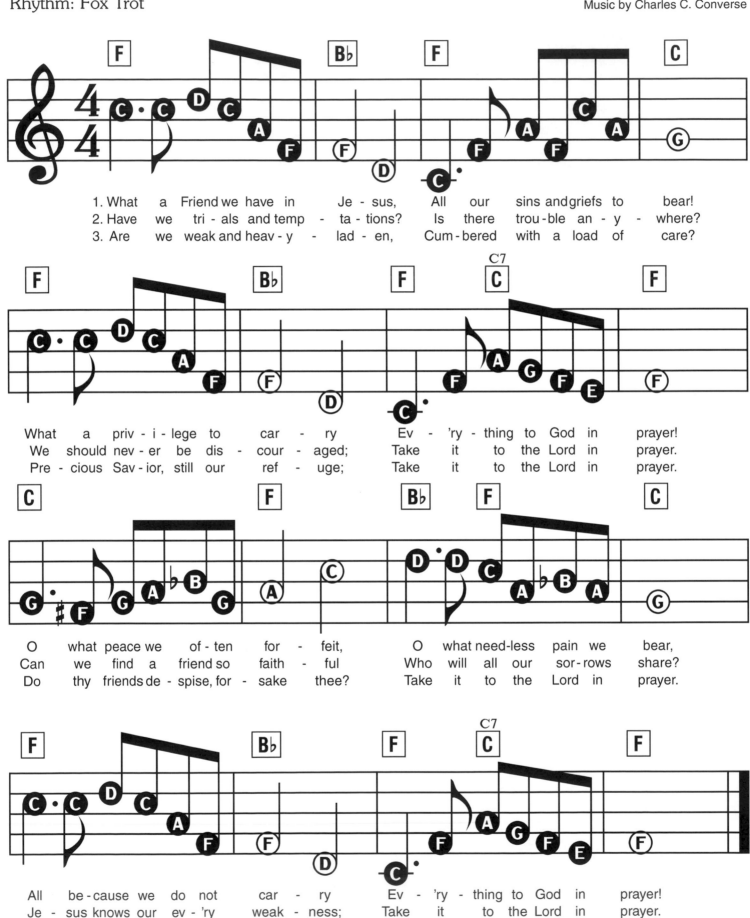

I Want to Stroll Over Heaven with You

Registration 2
Rhythm: Waltz

Words and Music by
J.B. Lemley

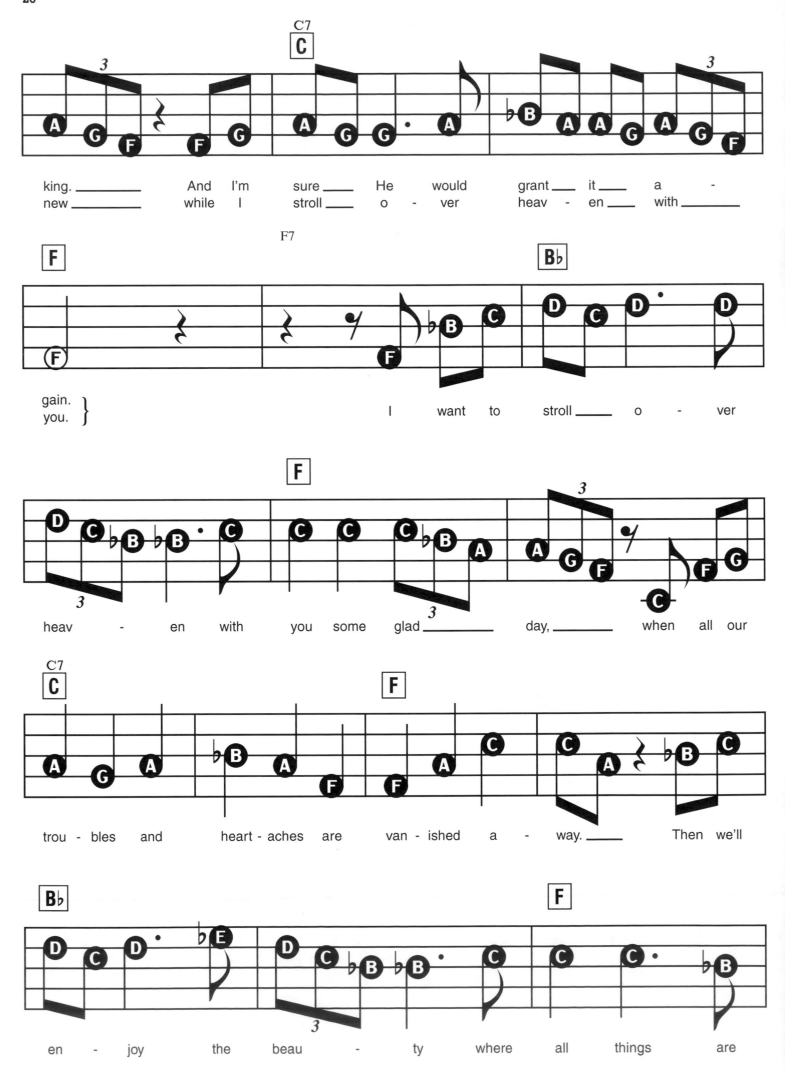

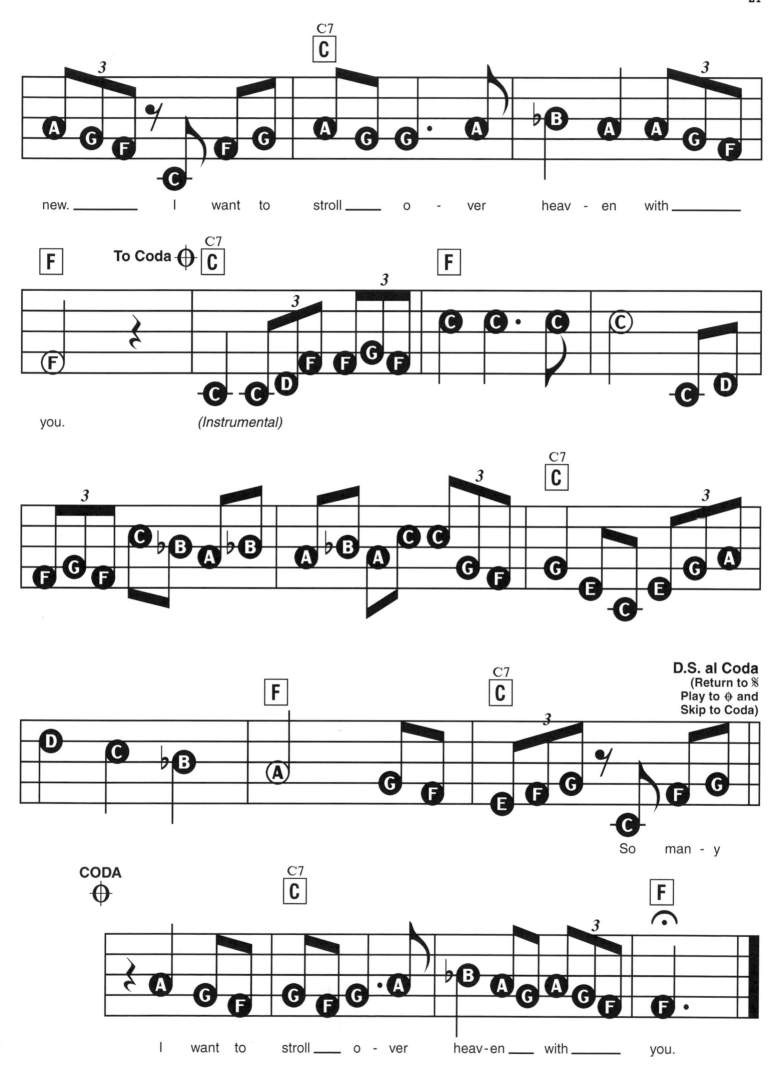

new. _____ I want to stroll _____ o - ver heav - en with _____

you.　　　　　　(Instrumental)

So man - y

I want to stroll _____ o - ver heav-en _____ with _____ you.

Standing on the Promises

Registration 5
Rhythm: March or Swing

Words and Music by
R. Kelso Carter

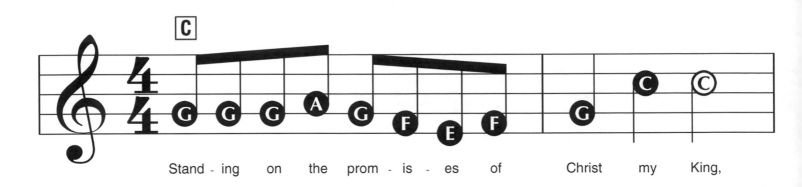

Stand - ing on the prom - is - es of Christ my King,

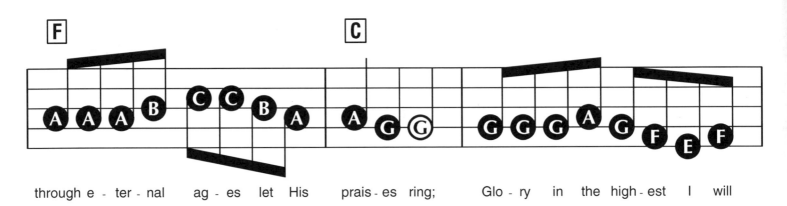

through e - ter - nal ag - es let His prais - es ring; Glo - ry in the high - est I will

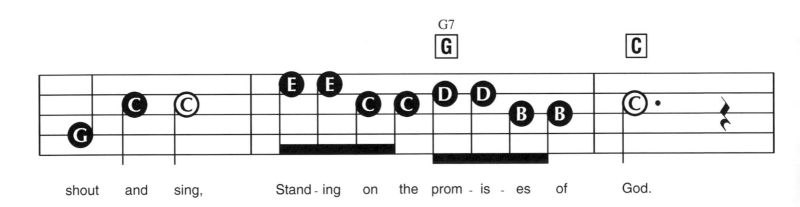

shout and sing, Stand - ing on the prom - is - es of God.

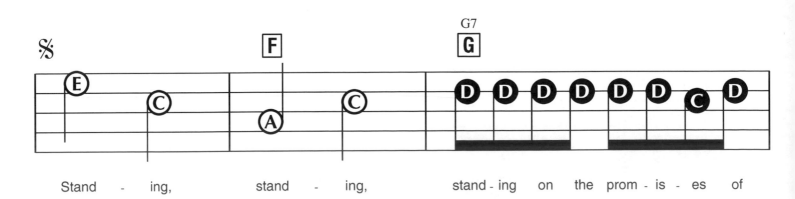

Stand - ing, stand - ing, stand - ing on the prom - is - es of

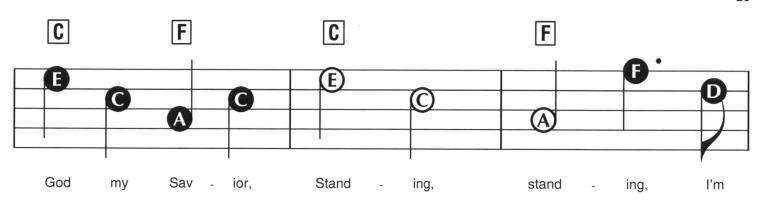

God my Sav - ior, Stand - ing, stand - ing, I'm

Fine

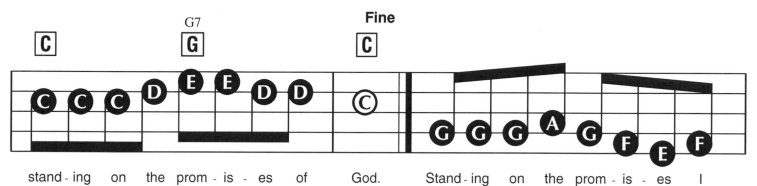

stand - ing on the prom - is - es of God. Stand - ing on the prom - is - es I

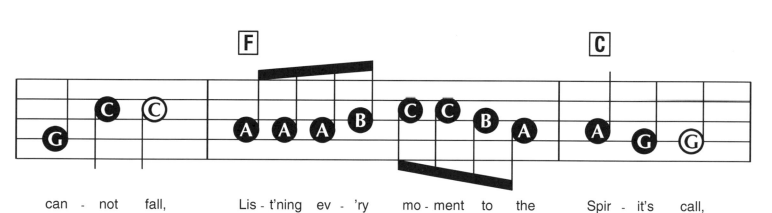

can - not fall, Lis - t'ning ev - 'ry mo - ment to the Spir - it's call,

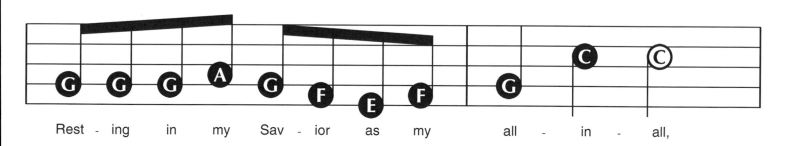

Rest - ing in my Sav - ior as my all - in - all,

D.S. al Fine
(Return to %
Play to Fine)

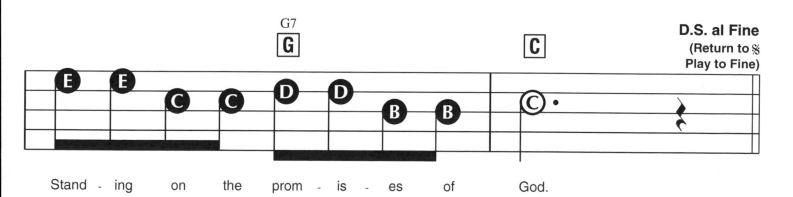

Stand - ing on the prom - is - es of God.

Turn Your Eyes Upon Jesus

Registration 8
Rhythm: Waltz

Words and Music by
Helen H. Lemmel

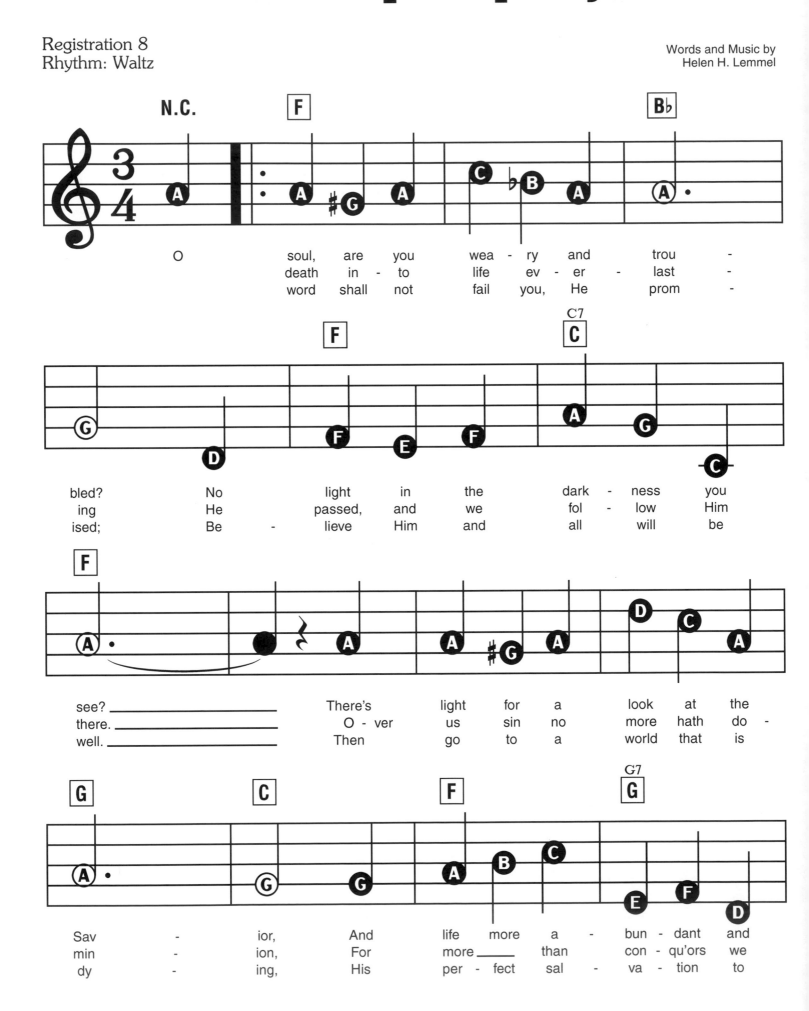

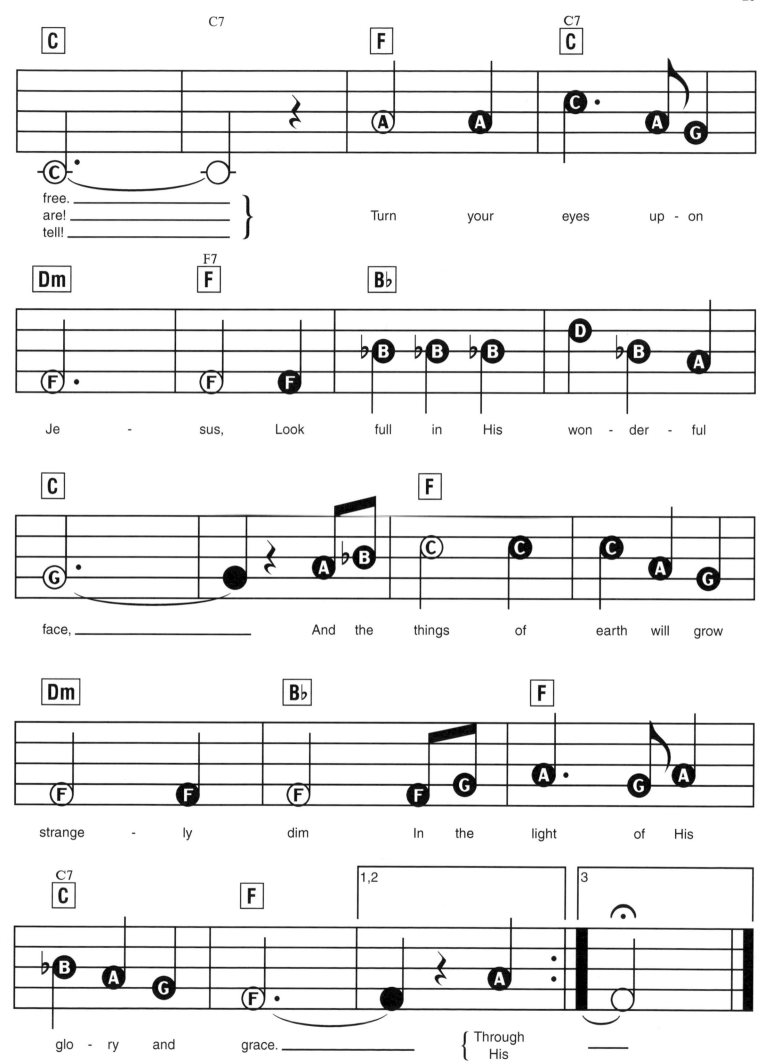

Leaning on the Everlasting Arms

Registration 7
Rhythm: March

Words by Elisha A. Hoffman
Music by Anthony J. Showalter

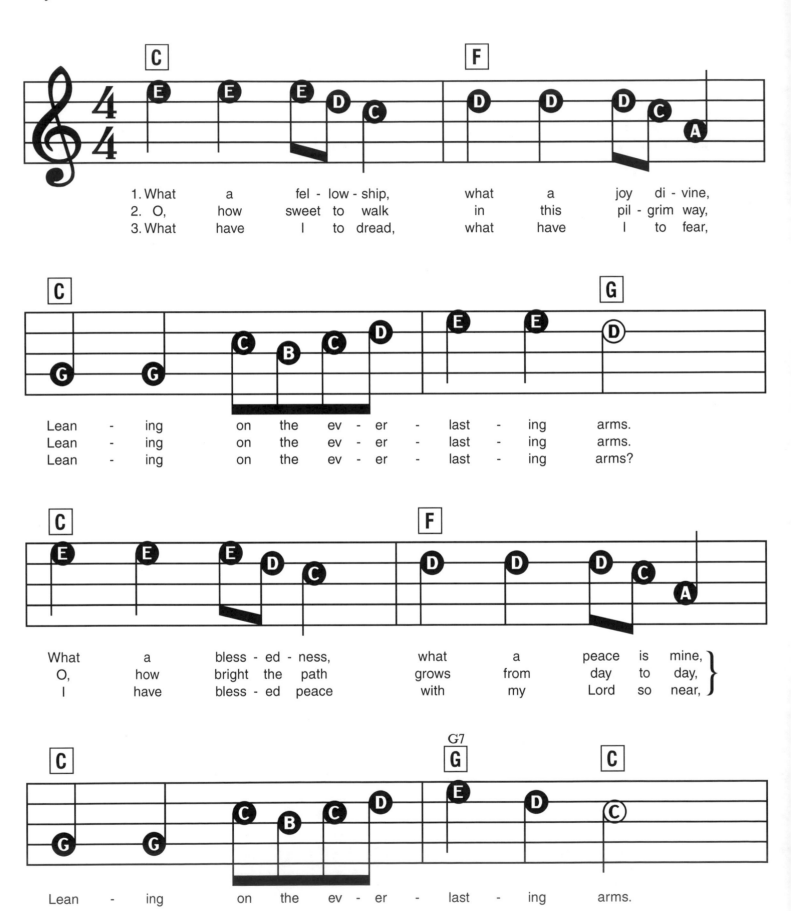

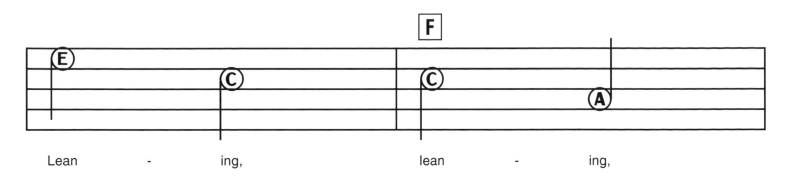

Lean - ing, lean - ing,

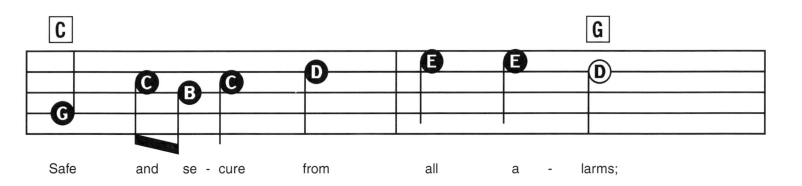

Safe and se - cure from all a - larms;

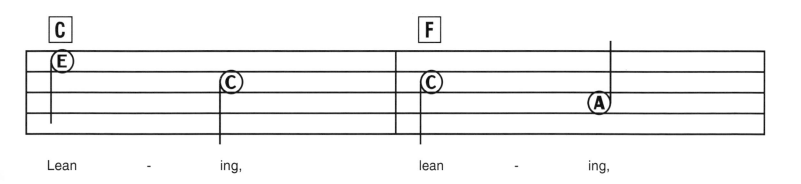

Lean - ing, lean - ing,

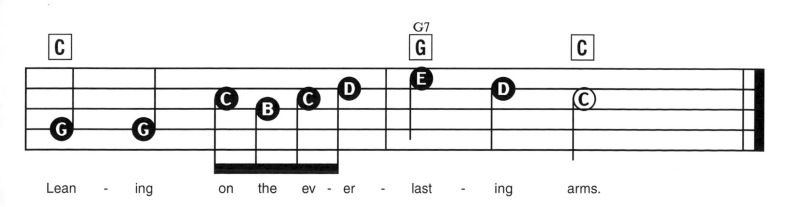

Lean - ing on the ev - er - last - ing arms.

The Old Rugged Cross

Registration 2
Rhythm: Waltz

Words and Music by
Rev. George Bennard

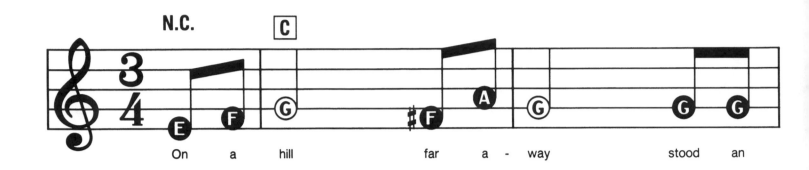

On a hill far a - way stood an

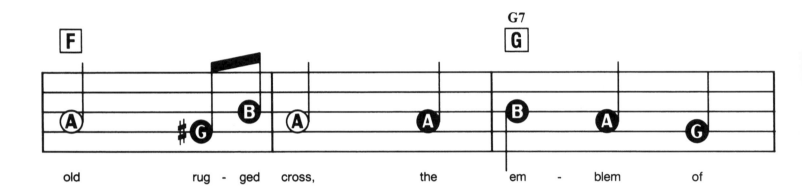

old rug - ged cross, the em - blem of

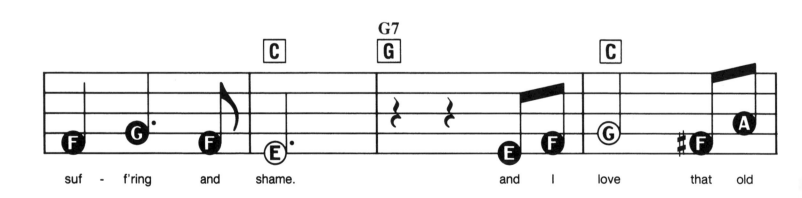

suf - f'ring and shame. and I love that old

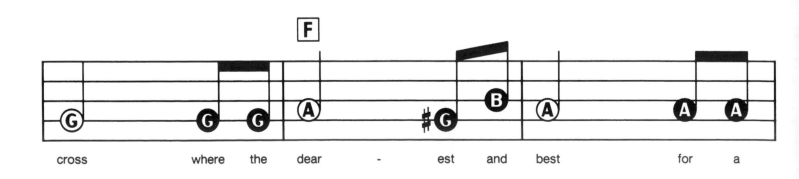

cross where the dear - est and best for a

29

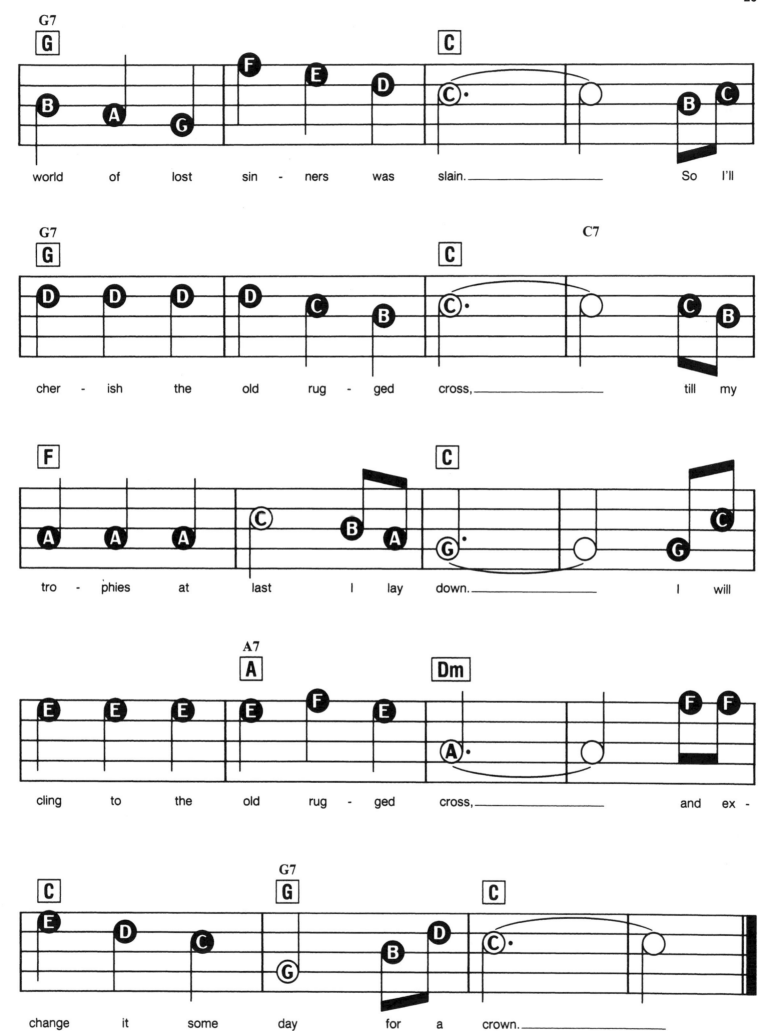

How Great Thou Art

Registration 6
Rhythm: None

Words and Music by
Stuart K. Hine

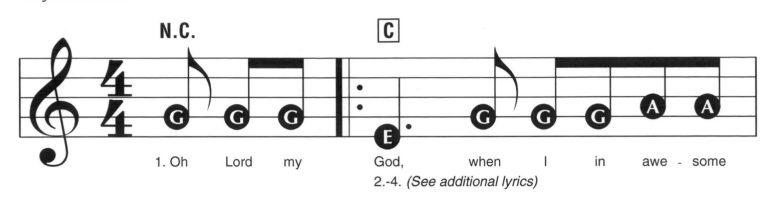

1. Oh Lord my God, when I in awe - some
2.-4. *(See additional lyrics)*

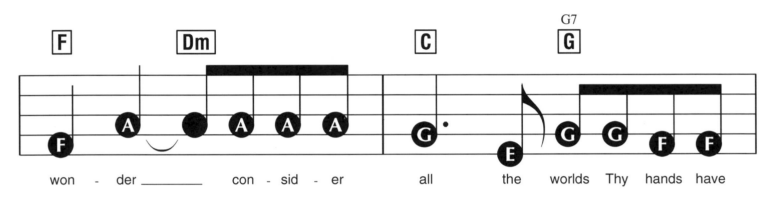

won - der _____ con - sid - er all the worlds Thy hands have

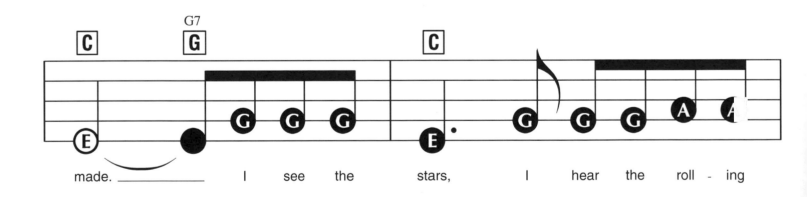

made. _____ I see the stars, I hear the roll - ing

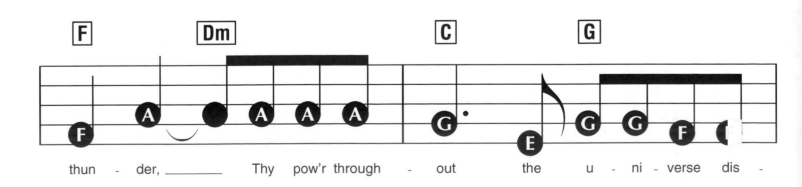

thun - der, _____ Thy pow'r through - out the u - ni - verse dis -

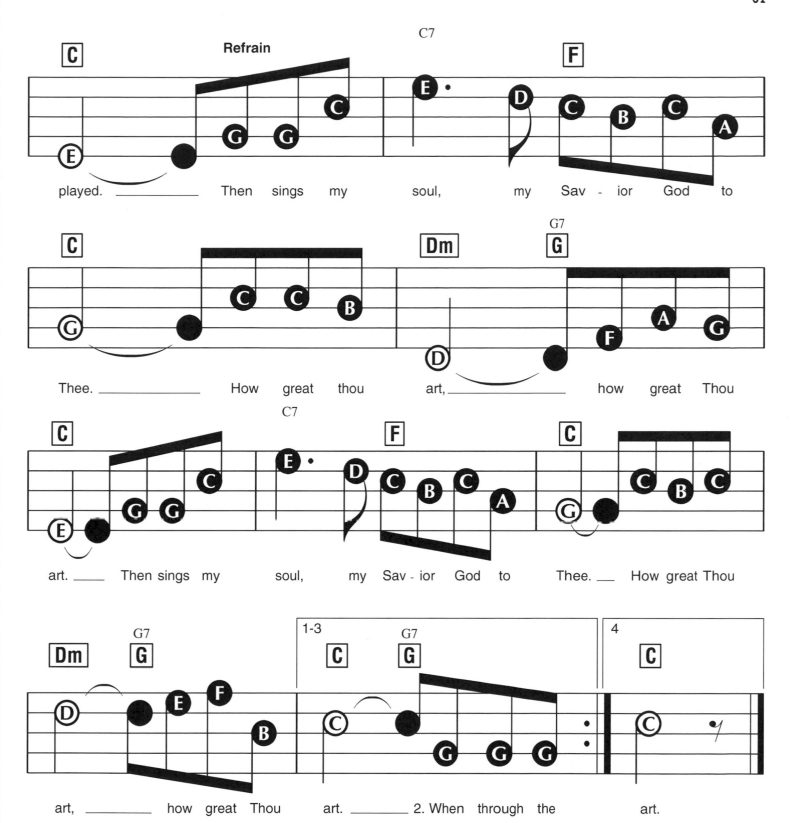

Additional Lyrics

2. When through the woods and forest glades I wander,
   And hear the birds sing sweetly in the trees.
   When I look down from lofty mountain grandeur,
   And hear the brook and feel the gentle breeze.

   Refrain

3. And when I think that God, His Son not sparing,
   Sent Him to die, I scarce can take it in.
   That on the cross, my burden gladly bearing,
   He bled and died to take away my sin.

   Refrain

4. When Christ shall come with shout of acclamation
   And take me home, what joy shall fill my heart!
   Then I shall bow in humble adoration
   And there proclaim my God how great Thou art.

   Refrain